Bryce's Blanket

Written by:
Claudia Harris

Illustrated by:
TullipStudio

Dedication

For everyone who encouraged or inspired me to make my own path. The trail has just begun..........

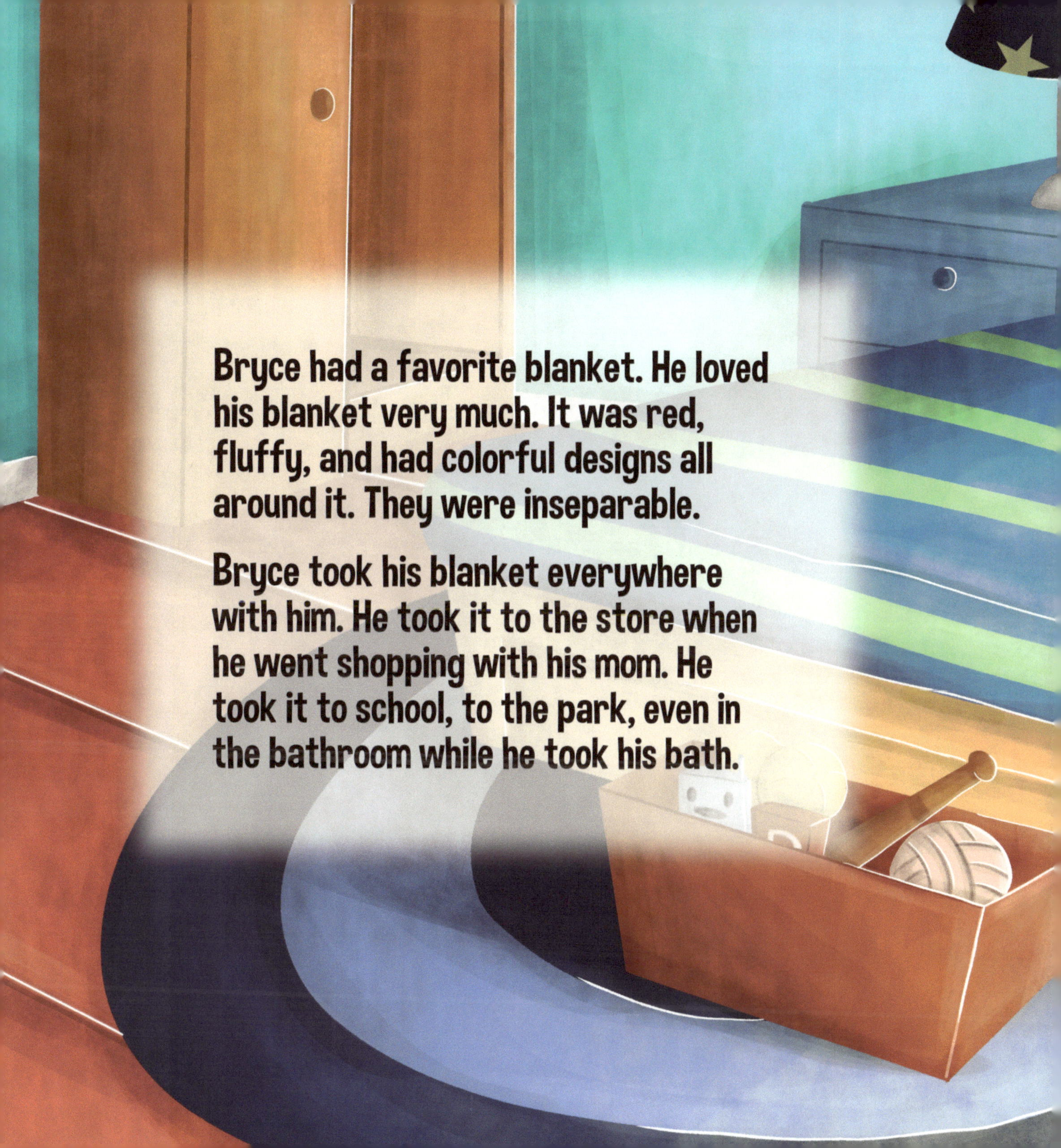

Bryce had a favorite blanket. He loved his blanket very much. It was red, fluffy, and had colorful designs all around it. They were inseparable.

Bryce took his blanket everywhere with him. He took it to the store when he went shopping with his mom. He took it to school, to the park, even in the bathroom while he took his bath.

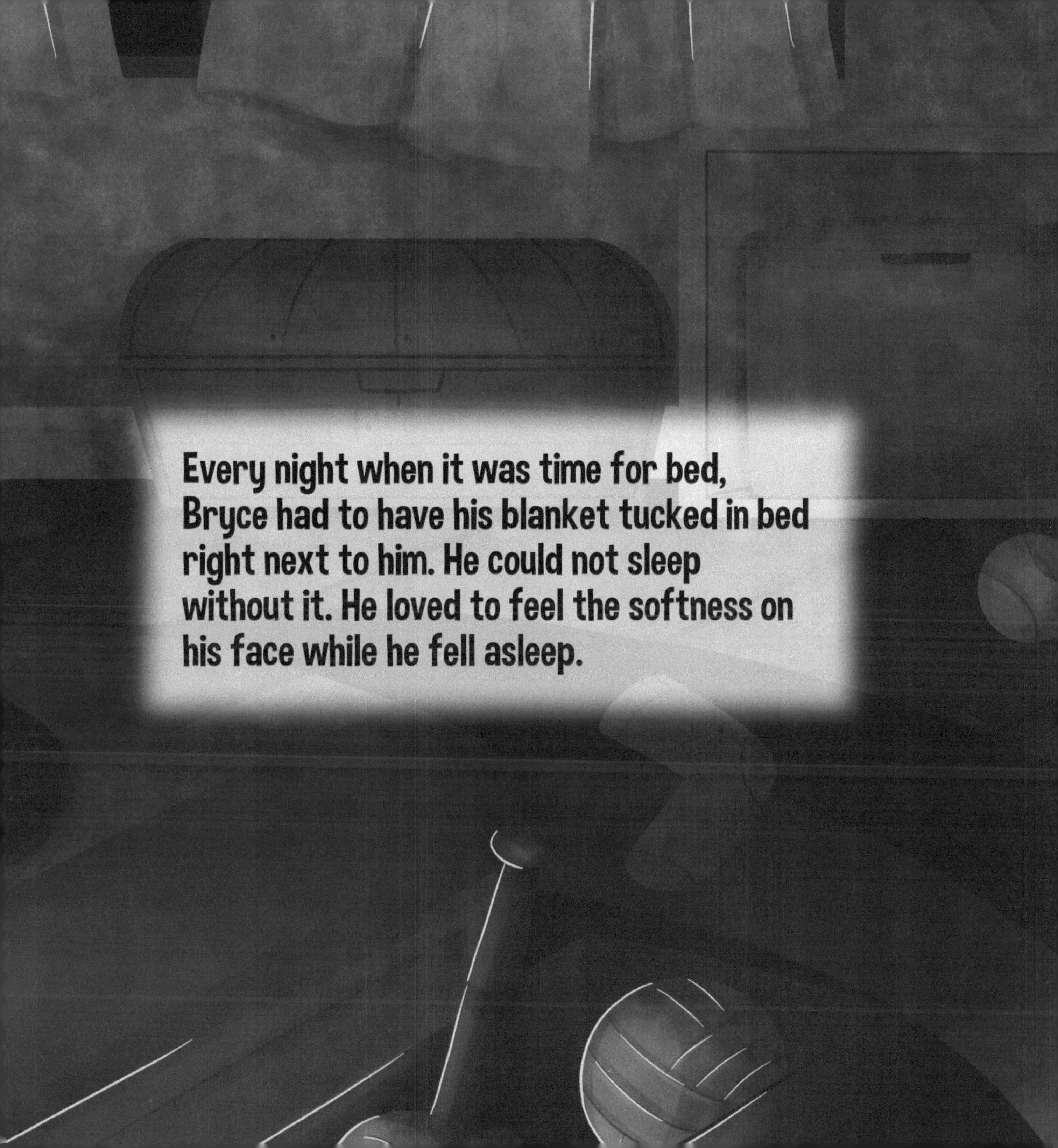
Every night when it was time for bed,
Bryce had to have his blanket tucked in bed
right next to him. He could not sleep
without it. He loved to feel the softness on
his face while he fell asleep.

One morning when Bryce woke up, his blanket was missing. He looked under the bed - no blanket. He looked between the sheets - no blanket. He looked under the pillows - still no blanket.

He looked in the bathroom - no blanket. He checked his parents' room - no blanket. He ran downstairs and looked under the sofa - still no blanket.

Bryce looked in the front yard, checked the car, and even looked inside the mailbox, but his blanket was not there.

B

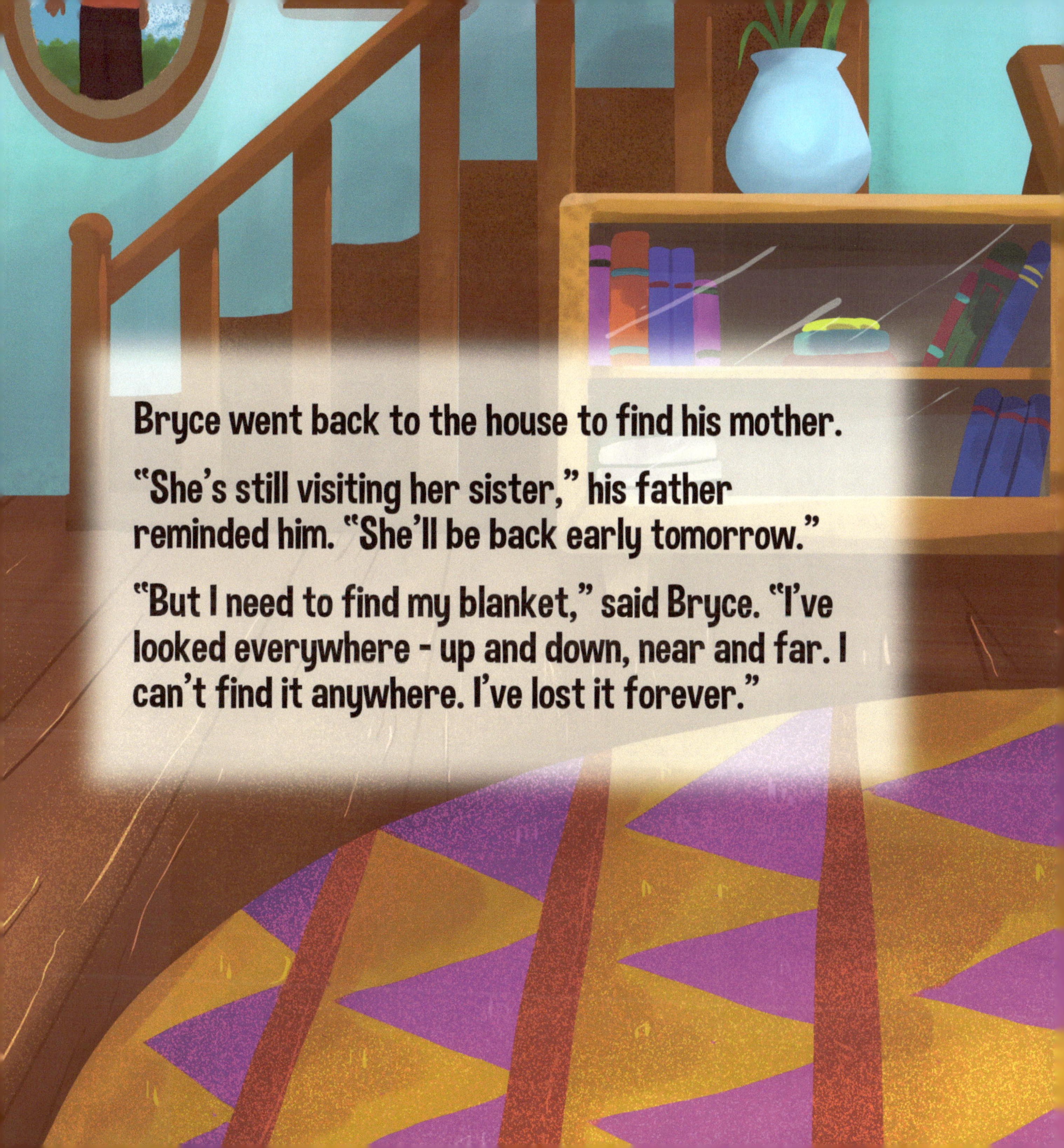

Bryce went back to the house to find his mother.

"She's still visiting her sister," his father reminded him. "She'll be back early tomorrow."

"But I need to find my blanket," said Bryce. "I've looked everywhere - up and down, near and far. I can't find it anywhere. I've lost it forever."

Bryce's dad helped him look.
They looked all day until it was bedtime.
But they couldn't find Bryce's blanket.

That night, Bryce tossed and turned because he was not used to sleeping without his blanket. Every time he started drifting off asleep, he would reach to feel the softness of his blanket and would remember that it was gone.

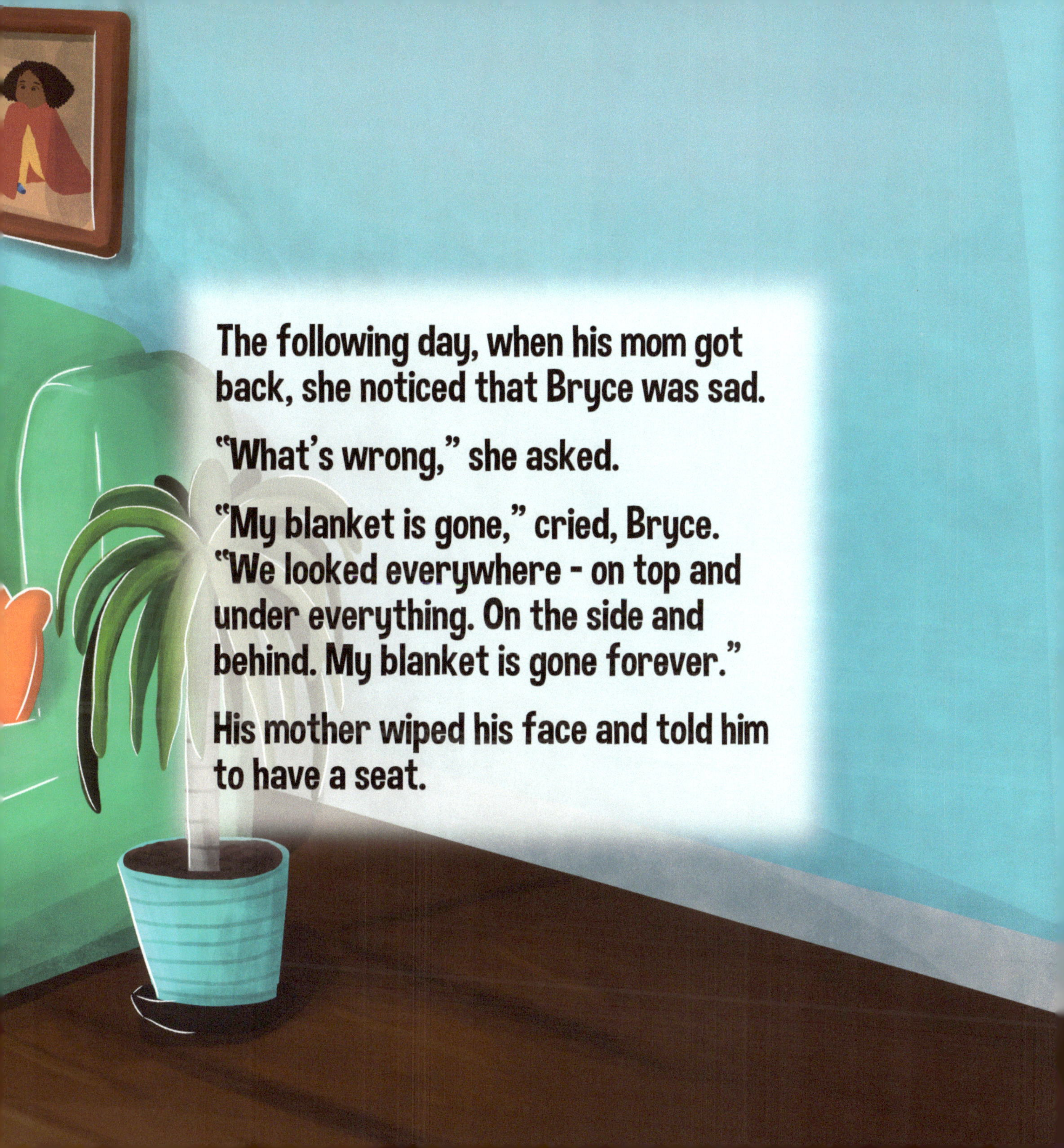

The following day, when his mom got back, she noticed that Bryce was sad.

"What's wrong," she asked.

"My blanket is gone," cried, Bryce. "We looked everywhere - on top and under everything. On the side and behind. My blanket is gone forever."

His mother wiped his face and told him to have a seat.

She walked away, and when she returned, she was holding his favorite blanket.

"Mom, you found it!" Bryce yelled. He was so happy to have his blanket back.

"I washed it yesterday morning," his mom said, "and it was still in the dryer."

Bryce smiled and hugged his mom, holding onto his favorite red fluffy blanket with all its colorful designs.

The End

Bryce's Blanket Activity

What is your favorite toy or item?

Draw a picture or write a sentence about your favorite thing.